Falling in Love with me

A Personal Journey and a Guide to Falling in Love With You

Marcy Morrison *a.k.a.* Tinkerangel

Kayrie. Here's to loving you. Marcy

Tinkerangel
San Diego, California
www.tinkerangel.com
858.213.5945

Cover Design & Illustration: Matt Hinrichs
Interior Layout: Ruth Schwartz—custom design based on template from BookDesignTemplates.com

Ordering Information:
Quantity sales. Special discounts are available on quantity purchases by corporations, associations, and others. For details, contact the "Special Sales Department" at marcy@tinkerangel.com.

Falling In Love With ME/Marcy Morrison. — 1st ed.
ISBN 978-1-4959536-5-1

My Journey – Falling in Love With ME

I N THE FALL OF 2012, I had a vision. A man who appeared to be my soulmate came to me and said, "I will not be able to come to you until you fall in love with you." He said, "It is very important that you keep a journal called Falling in Love with ME" – meaning myself – not him (just to clarify). So I did just that – never thinking that this would become the title of my next book and would help others fall in love with themselves. The Universe definitely sent me on quite an adventure since that vision, and I will be honest, some of it was not pretty. But it was all necessary to heal old wounds from childhood and release/shed old behaviors and relationships that no longer served me. I received many blessings and gifts on this journey in the form of beautiful souls who serendipitously appeared to help me learn to fall in love with myself, who held my hand when those moments of deep sadness and pain appeared, as well of those moments of feeling lost and hopeless. They held the light for me in my darkness and I am forever grateful for them. If you need their help on this journey, there is a resource section at the end of this book where some of these magical people are listed.

This book was also inspired by the many career/life coaching clients I have worked with. I have seen so many successful people who, according to our society, appear to have it all but feel completely unfulfilled. What I have realized for myself, for my clients and for others is this: If you are not in love with yourself first, you will never be fulfilled. You can continue to chase happiness, achievements and recognition, but it will all be meaningless – until you fall in love with you.

Part of my discovery through falling in love with me was how I didn't share all of myself with the world. I realized that this was due to a challenging childhood where it was too scary to fully express myself, as well as my fear of what people/society would think. On this journey, I found out that I am here on this earth to be me. Being me is allowing the playful, fun, creative part of me out, which my friends call "Tinkerangel." It has been so liberating to let Tinkerangel out of the closet that I decided to let the Tinkerangel part of me write this book. So be prepared for some fun in bringing out your inner child who remembers who you really are. I do have to warn you though that falling in love with you doesn't mean that it is all fun. It means shedding what no longer serves you, which can be incredibly painful and sad sometimes. But I promise that there is light at the end of the tunnel.

Marcy as Tinkerangel
(tinkerangel.com)

I will share with you the steps I took to fall in love with me – and stay in love with me – through the following chapters called **"L — O — V — E"**:

1. **L — Let Yourself Find Out Who You Are**

2. **O — Open Yourself to Allow More In of What You Want**

3. **V — Value and Appreciate and Honor Who You Are Every Day**

4. **E — Enjoy and Express You**

So now let's begin the journey together . . .

CHAPTER 1

"𝓛" – Let Yourself Find Out Who You Are

OK, I HAVE TO FOREWARN YOU . . . this self-discovery part can be intense, so be prepared for the ride and get the help, love and support you need along the way. And here is a word to the wise – don't rush through this book. Yes, I know you can blow through a little book like this in no time, but that is not its purpose. The point is to go deep, especially into this first chapter – and take as long as you need. As you can see from my story, it was at least a year-long process. While a lot of healing and shedding had been happening prior, 2013 in particular was a keystone year of *falling in love with ME*. So please take your time in the process of *falling in love with YOU* – you are worth the time.

In the beginning of 2013, life was not working for me. I had recently gone through a divorce after being married for 14 years (we were together a total of 17 years). The year before my divorce, I had decided that I needed to close my coaching business and get a "job" while I moved through the transition. I kept picking one wrong opportunity after another. I was feeling drained by my friendships and no longer had the energy to be the social coordinator and the one who helped everyone. Finally, I cried "mercy" and declared to the Universe: *I obviously don't have it figured out and I need your help so I surrender my life to you.* Shortly after, during a meditation, I had a vision. A Native American Chief knelt down on one knee and handed me a peace pipe and said, "Congratulations as you enter into the next leg of your journey." In that moment, I knew I needed to work with Native Americans, but where? I started putting feelers out and I was led to work with Barbara Korte, an incredible woman in Sedona. I shared with her that I felt it was important that I work with a Native American. She said, "Just this morning I saw Joseph White Wolf – maybe you are meant to work with him."

During my session with Joseph, he shared my *totems* with me that were revealed to him in his *Dreamtime*. This was extremely insightful in helping me heal and uncover who I am and why I am here. One key totem that Joseph shared with me was the maple tree. He said, "When you look at the maple tree, you don't see it rip

itself out of the ground by its roots and go chasing anything, do you? No, because the maple tree knows that
its sweetness is inside, and whatever is meant to come to
it, will." Joseph probably had no idea how profound
and impactful that statement would be for me. I had
spent so much of my life chasing people and opportunities, trying to make things happen. Much of that
stemmed from fear and low self-esteem. Joseph helped
me get grounded in knowing that I am enough, and
what is meant to come to me, will. That was a huge step
in self-love for me and has brought me so much more
peace and trust in allowing my journey to unfold as it
was meant to unfold.

**Joseph White Wolf in Sedona at a crystal bed sharing with
me my totems that he saw in his _Dreamtime._**

Working with Joseph also led me back to Jesse Gros, a friend who I decided to hire as my coach. I highly recommend working with a coach or some other professional who can guide you through the rocky waters you may encounter. Jesse really helped me shed what no longer served me and challenged me to express all parts of myself. Jesse also encouraged me to keep a daily journal of whatever I was experiencing. He *knew* that my journey would be put into a book. I am so thankful for Jesse, for that encouragement, since many stories in this book came from that journal.

Jesse, me and Joseph
Yes, it is crazy how much Jesse and Joseph look alike. The Universe sent me two similar looking angels to help me on my journey.

Growing up in a challenging home, part of the role I assumed was to appear that I was always positive, strong and I had it all figured out. Jesse helped me give myself permission to not always have to appear positive and to be able to express all of my emotions, including pain and sadness. I had to look deep into what were the roles that I assumed from childhood or from society that weren't really me, and then have the courage to walk away from those roles. I got so wrapped up in my identity of always being positive, always helping others, always being the social coordinator and always looking like I had it figured it out.

Letting this all go was overwhelming at first. I felt lost – like *who am I* if I am not all of these things? I also let go of friends who weren't able to be there for me as I shed all of these ways of being. It was difficult and lonely at times. I had to sit in the void, pain and sadness for a while as I let go of the old and found out who I really was. Jesse also helped me move from always being in my head trying to figure everything out to a place of "feeling it out," where I connect to my heart and intuition. This made me much happier and allowed me to have a deep trust and respect for myself. I learned to honor myself by really listening to my internal guidance and what I want to do in each moment.

I had to look at why I kept picking all the wrong people and the wrong opportunities. Through working with Jesse and also reading an amazing book that I highly recommend called *The Presence Process*, I could see that I was reliving old patterns from childhood. With my parents mostly unavailable, I kept picking unavailable people and opportunities. Along with this was a deep subconscious belief that I didn't deserve abundance and love, and there was definitely a part of me that didn't honor, love and respect myself. So I went deep into this, and with the love and support of my coach and friends, I felt the pain and sadness and loneliness. I also realized that I had to go into that pain and sadness to integrate what I never was able, or allowed myself, to feel as a child and throughout my life. For me, I needed this time to integrate old unintegrated emotions. I love what *The Presence Process* says, "We aren't trying to feel good, we get better at feeling." When I came out on the other side, I felt a deep love, honor and respect for myself and realized that I had to first start with that because if I don't love, honor and respect myself, how can I expect this from others? I also came out the other side a more fully authentic human being. I am more vulnerable and able to express all of myself. I no longer expect myself to appear positive, happy and having it all figured out all the time. I unconditionally love and accept myself wherever I am in each moment. In being able to do this, I am much better at being able to do this for others. I also let go of all the unavailable friends and became better at choosing healthier opportunities and people. I stopped being so needy and trying to find love and happiness from outside of myself. I found what I needed inside of me.

Let's look at you:
- Is your life working?

  o Why?

  o Why not?

  o What would it look like to you if it were working?

  o What do you need to shed that is no longer serving you?

    - Physical belongings

    - Ways of being

    - Friendships

I realized that I never felt like I was "enough." I never felt pretty or smart enough. I felt like I never did enough. I also saw this with my clients. I had one client that was convinced that he was worthless unless he got a bachelor's degree. We turned that around with him knowing that he is enough right now, because the truth is, if he didn't realize it right now, he would get the bachelor's degree and then there would be another thing that would make him feel like he is not enough. It was the same for me – one more degree, a boyfriend, traveling, people 24/7 telling me how amazing I am, the perfect job – would not make me feel like enough. The feeling of *enough-ness* had to come from within me.

I worked with another client who had so many of what our society considers "success" boxes checked off. He had two master's degrees from prestigious universities, was financially successful, built and owned multiple businesses, owned homes, traveled the world and was married with a child. But when he came to me, he was lifeless, passionless and unfulfilled. Why? Didn't he have it all? He had on the outside what society would say is everything, but not on the inside. When we dug deeper, we found out that he carried around a deep subconscious belief from his childhood that no matter what he did or accomplished, in his mom's eyes, it was *never enough*. So he kept the endless chase of *trying to be enough* going. We began working on him knowing that he was enough and truly finding himself at age 45. That meant finding out what he loved to do, what made him happy and letting go of what anyone else thought of him. This brought him great peace and a deep level of fulfillment that he had never experienced in his life before.

- What stories do you tell yourself about not being enough?

- Could you see that you are enough right now? How are you enough right now?

- What do you love about yourself right now?

- What are you proud of right now?

- Who would you be without your childhood baggage, without whatever society or anyone else wants you to be?

In the past, I had a history of keeping myself constantly busy doing things. How can we find ourselves when we are so busy? I remember the feeling of despair the first night alone in my new apartment after I separated from my husband. I was so used to a busy house with husband, kids and animals. I felt so alone and I didn't like it. In time, I learned the beauty of being alone and in silence. I learned that I can refill my tank and love my own company during these times of solitude, so that when I am again with other people, I have more to give since I have filled myself up with so much love for myself. In this silence, I would get and continue to receive many drops of wisdom about myself and the world. I found it very helpful to take at least 15 minutes each morning and night to be quiet and listen to my higher self and my inner child. In doing this, I found the parts of me I had lost while being too busy and being who I thought I was supposed to be for others.

For me, it is most powerful to be in nature at the beach. I have a very special beach that I go to near where I live and I can instantly feel myself becoming grounded there. My head stops spinning and I get very still. Wisdom pours into me when I am in this spot. The inspiration for this book came to me there as did many other insights, poetry and ideas. You too can find your own magical spot that speaks to you.

Me at my magical spot

As a coach, I find that whatever I say to my clients is usually exactly what I need to hear for myself. So often, my clients become way too serious about life and forget to have fun and play. I realized that I also had gotten too serious and forgot how to play. I had to really slow down and get to know myself and ask myself, *what is it that I like to do, what is fun for me?* Fortunately, I have two young children so they help me immensely in remembering how to have fun, be childlike and celebrate wonder. I remember being in my serious adult mode one day, focused on getting somewhere and my kids stopped to look at a mushroom as we were on our way to the car. They said, "Hey Mom, check out this really cool mushroom," as they lay down on the ground to get a really good look. I said, "I don't have time for that. We need to be somewhere." They gave me this look like, *Really, Mom – you don't have time to check out this miraculous thing in nature?* That stopped me in my tracks and I heard in my head, *yes you have time to look at this mushroom and you have time to slow down more and find the wonder in everything and enjoy it all the time just like a child.* By slowing down and enjoying each moment, being present in each moment, I find such a deeper fulfillment in my life and this helps me love ME and love my life even more.

My beautiful boys Cameron and Logan, and me

Another discovery: In the quiet, silence and in moments of play, it was almost as if everything appeared as if spring had come and beautiful bright flowers were blossoming everywhere. I became more aware of:

- **My Intuition** – I was able to hear my inner voice and guidance so much more clearly when I got quiet.

- **My Creativity**
  - **Painting** – I discovered how much I enjoy painting and now my room is filled with my paintings. How fun!
  - **Poetry** – I started meditating at my favorite beach in San Diego whenever possible and many times poetry would just start coming to me. I didn't know I could create like this before. Here is my first poem that I received on my *falling in love with me* journey:

Sprinkling Sunshine

Love fills my heart entering into every crevice of my body
Flowing like a river nourishing my soul
Gentle waves of happiness shine their smiles upon me
Sunshine sprinkling down illuminating the path ahead
Stillness, peace, the unraveling of what was to allow in what is meant to be
A dove whispers – know who you are and shine that bright light for the whole world to see

- **My Healing Abilities** – I also began to realize that not only was I an intuitive coach, but that I also was being given guidance on how to help others heal.

- **My Playfulness**
  - ○ **Hula Hooping** – I began to incorporate more really fun things into my day, like hula hooping. I also decided to share this fun with others and began bringing a hula hoop and other forms of creative expression into my workshops and coaching.

When you get quiet and go to your magical spot – what gifts will you find within you that you forgot or had never discovered? What else will you find out about yourself?

Another key piece of *falling in love with me* was to go deep into forgiving myself and others. Once I let go of the burdens of carrying around anger and resentment towards myself and others, so much more space was cleared out of me, creating the space for unconditional love for myself and others.

I also found it really important to look for the gems amidst the challenges I faced in my life and how they could help me with who I am and what I do today. I realized that someone once called me a "weaver," meaning a person who helps weave together others' passions and life stories to help them find their purpose and create meaning and passion in their lives. I have also had to do this for myself.

- From growing up in a challenging environment, I learned to develop a great compassion for others and a desire to hold my hand out to help pull other people out of their darkness. I don't think I could do this at the depth that I do if I hadn't experienced deep pain, sadness and suffering in my life and then found my way through it.

- I used to get upset that I wasn't able to figure out my passion and purpose from day one and that I have had many different careers. I have come to realize that this has helped me be a better coach, having walked so many different paths.

I remember being so hard on myself and thinking, *when am I going to figure it out*? Then I realized that there were points in my life when I did have the courage to be me and follow my heart even when others said I was crazy. For example, I decided to be an exchange student from New Jersey to Australia during my last year of high school. Everyone said, "How can you leave your senior year, prom and graduation?" Something inside of me – *a calling* – told me that it was much more important to be an exchange student in Australia than it was to stay in New Jersey for my senior year. It is definitely something I have never regretted. It was a life changing experience for me that truly broadened my horizons and changed the course of what I have done with my life. When I took the time to celebrate experiences like this, it gave me the strength to have the courage to step more into being me and to not be afraid to be and express who I really am.

- At what points in your life did you have the courage to be truly you?

- What moments are you most proud of?

My Light at the End of the Tunnel

I wrote the following as the light started to enter the darkness and I could feel a shift:

I am falling in love with who I am. I can feel it strongly today and I am excited about who I am and what I have to offer. No wonder I was lost – I had to find myself, learn to love myself and truly honor and respect myself. I feel the creativity flowing from me. I am connecting to people who like to do what I love to do and I am ready now to receive from others – abundance and opportunities – because I know that I deserve that and it is part of the flow of life. I cannot only just give. I must also receive. I have always been good about giving – now I am learning to become good at receiving. I feel my strength returning and a real desire to get out there and do what I am meant to do. I feel very confident and not afraid to show the Tinkerangel part of myself. I am so grateful that I hired Jesse for this work. I feel that this journey of finding myself will only help others more. It has been a very difficult and painful journey at times, but I am so grateful for the shedding of that which no longer serves me.

- Write your light at the end of the tunnel story.

CHAPTER 2

"O" ~ Open Yourself to Allowing More In of What You Want

W HAT IS IT THAT YOU REALLY WANT?
How do we move past the stories that we
tell ourselves and stop being so serious? I
found it very helpful for me to get creative
and playful and step into character – a character that
represents my higher self, who I really am. However, I
was still having difficulty expressing myself fully due to
fear of what others may think. My character is Tinkerangel. I know I am meant to bring more joy, playfulness, creativity and fun to this world and help others
uncover who they really are and why they are here. OK,
I know you have been thinking, *what is the deal with*

this Tinkerangel thing? How does one even come up with something like that? While on my journey of *falling in love with ME*, the more I expressed who I really am, one of my favorite friends, Amanda, came up with the nickname *Tinkerangel* for me. Amanda is one of those friends that I feel fully free to be completely *ME* when I am around her. She helped me express the Tinkerangel part of myself and I highly recommend that you surround yourself with those types of friends. She told me, "You are like a little fairy that goes around and sprinkles happy joy dust on everyone to help them express who they really are. You are an angel who deeply cares about others and wants to help them – you are a *Tinkerangel*." We both went dead silent and said, "Whoa – that IS who I really am." I am forever grateful to Amanda for helping me see and develop and express that part of me.

Amanda and Marcy at the magical spot.

I also have to thank my coach/friend Jesse. As we started working together he said, "I know there is this really juicy part of you that I really want to get to know and I am intrigued. What is that part of you?" I thought for a moment and I said, *you mean that Tinkerangel part of me?* Jesse said, "That sounds interesting, tell me more." I described the Tinkerangel side of me and he said, "Yes, I want to see you express more of Tinkerangel in your life – that is why you are here for yourself and others." Interestingly, Jesse had me go through the process of cleaning out my physical belongings right after we spoke about this. One thing I had to do was untangle all of my jewelry that was just in a messy ball. In this tangled mess, out popped this charm that looked like Tinkerangel. I started to cry as I realized what a powerful symbol this exercise was in my journey to *falling in love with ME* – untangling all of the layers of what I thought I was supposed to be and allowing myself to be who I really am – *Tinkerangel.*

Now let's begin the process of untangling you and finding out who you really are via your character. I suggest finding a quiet spot in nature if possible, or just a quiet spot in general. Give yourself at least an hour to work through this. If you get stuck, I highly recommend finding a friend like Amanda or an amazing coach like Jesse to help you see what you may not see in yourself.

- Who is your character? Does your character have a name? Some of my clients have used characters or people whom they felt represented who they really were such as: Wonder Woman, the Dalai Lama, a rock star, Pocahontas, Woody from *Toy Story*, etc.

- Describe the qualities of your character. What are the parts of yourself that you feel are the juicy parts of you that you really want to express and share with the world?

- When is your character the happiest?

- How does your character enjoy spending his/her time?
  - For example – outside, helping others, traveling, reading a book, etc. List everything your character loves.

- What does your character enjoy doing?

  - Type of work

  - Type of play

  - Other adventures

- What dreams does your character have for himself/herself?

- What dreams do you have for the world?

- How can you make these dreams come true?

- What is fun for you?

- What did you find fun as a child that you wish you could go back and do now?

- Do you create enough time in your life for fun now? If no, why? What is blocking you?

- How can you create more fun in your life and in each day?

- How can you share your fun with other people?

- What does your character feel like it is good at doing?

- What parts of yourself do you feel like you hide from the world that you would like to express more of?

- What does your perfect world look like?

- What can you do to help contribute to making this a perfect world?

- Ask your character what else it would like to share with you.

- Summarize your findings from above.

- Draw a picture of your character, and then around your character, draw all of the things your character loves.

In addition to what you discovered, think about what else you want to create in your life and also look at what you already have, but maybe have not noticed. For example, here are some highlights of what I realized that I wanted to create in my life or what was already in my life that I wasn't noticing or taking the time to be deeply grateful for:

Loving Supportive Friends

- I realized that I wanted to spend more time with friends who are loving, supportive, consistent, reliable and authentic, just as I showed up in my friendships. Then I realized that, while I had a lot of these types of friends in my life, I was choosing to spend my time chasing the unavailable ones. When I shifted my focus to my available friends, I felt this was an incredible way to love and honor myself. Here is an example of another amazing shift: One friend that I let go of during my time of shedding and transformation later came back to me and she didn't have any judgment. She loved me completely and unconditionally. Our friendship only grew stronger after I went through this process. I saw what a true friend she was by her allowing me the space and time to go on the journey I needed to go on and by not taking it personally. What an incredible example of unconditional friendship and love – thank you friend ☺.

The Ability to See and Receive Compliments

- I used to feel really uncomfortable receiving compliments, but the more I felt better about myself and loved myself, the better I was able to receive compliments. The beautiful part is that I never went around looking for compliments or expecting them, but it was almost like people sensed I was ready to receive them. I began to have people coming to me out of the blue saying how for years they always really admired my courage to do certain things, how they always thought I was so beautiful or whatever the compliment may be. When I stopped trying to be loved and simply loved myself, the more love came to me and I was more able to receive it.

Unconditionally Loving Myself

- Of course, just because you come to a place of unconditionally loving yourself doesn't mean that more healing and transformation doesn't need to take place or that life won't throw you curve balls to test how much you truly love yourself unconditionally. I had another profound moment during this process when I was in a yoga class and the teacher had us hug our knees in a gesture of hugging ourselves. I was completely overcome with emotion and started sobbing. I had always heard the expression that you will find someone who, when they hug you, all of your broken parts will come together. In that moment of hugging myself, I felt the experience of all of my broken parts coming together. I realized that I am that person, that I can do this for myself – and you can be that person that can do it for yourself.

Career

- I have always alternated between a traditional and non-traditional career. I realized that I am not meant for a traditional job. I am doing what I love and I know now that it is important for me to collaborate and work with others so I can make an even bigger impact.

Presence/Gratitude

- Neighborhood – I was always searching outside of myself and outside of where I am, but then I realized I have what I need within me and wherever I am in the moment. On this journey of *falling in love with ME* and grounding myself here and now, I got connected to my community and the local business owners in such an amazing way. I feel much more fulfilled, being truly present wherever I am now and so grateful for what I have right now.

Marcy with Cooper the Bird Rock Surf Shop dog, one of her best friends with whom she became very connected, upon slowing down and spending time in her neighborhood. His collar says, "I Love the Ladies," and oh yes, he does.

Marcy with Cooper and his baby boy Maverick – double the love at Bird Rock Surf Shop

Being with My Kids and Having More Fun

- I am now able to be much more present with my kids. I am truly enjoying our time together and learning from them how to see the world as a child again. I have regained my childlike wonderment and joy and I am now not afraid to express it. For example, my younger son and I went galloping around the toy store together on those stick horses. You should have seen the smile on his face –

amazed that his mom would play with him like that. We also made everyone's day in the store! I felt so happy to be free, have fun and express my childlike self. We can get so wrapped up in how we are *supposed to* behave. I know I did. I decided to not care and to simply behave how I want to behave (while being respectful). What is wrong with having more fun? ☺ Having more fun definitely allowed me to fall deeper in love with myself. I love my fun self. I like hanging out with my fun self and I see that it is magnetic. Others want to hang out with fun people and it gives them permission to have more fun.

Test riding horse and unicorn with my younger son Logan

Flow/Peace/Inner Guidance

• Travel has always been important to me and I have been very fortunate to have traveled to many places all over the world and within the United States. Before I had children, I used to travel a lot more, but I put extensive travel on hold while I raised my kids. But, when I got quiet, I kept feeling this pull to travel internationally. I feel happy when I think of traveling and doing work overseas because I love connecting with and learning from other cultures. I feel filled up when I travel. It challenges me and stretches me. It broadens my horizons. It expands me. It helps me see things in different ways. It energizes me. It recharges me. To me, travel is one of my most favorite things to do. Yet, I kept hearing, *it is really irresponsible for you as a mother to travel – you need to be here for your kids.* At the same time, I don't believe in the traditional system in the United States. While I have lived in it, I feel in my soul that there are other ways to raise/educate kids. When I see my American friends living and raising their kids while they work overseas, I feel so drawn to that. I know my kids would learn even more about themselves and the world by having international/multi-cultural experiences. As I was going through this journey of *falling in love with me* and getting clear on how important travel is to me, an opportunity fell into my lap to travel to the Amazon rainforest in Ecuador with the Pachamama Alliance (www.pachamama.org), to spend time with the indigenous people. I knew I had to go and said to myself, *"If I knock on all of the doors that I need to, in order to have this happen and they all open, then I will know I am meant to go."* All of the doors opened and it was such a perfect trip for me to integrate *falling in love with me*. It turned out that all of those voices I heard in my head about me being a bad mom for going were wrong. This trip not only inspired me, it inspired my children that their mom had the courage to go on such a life-changing adventure that was about doing good for the world.

Marcy with the children in the Sarayaku community in the Amazon rainforest in Ecuador

Ok, now it's your turn. Get quiet – listen to your heart – ask your heart for guidance – write down what your heart says. Now draw a picture of a heart and put all of that inside your heart and look at it every day. Tie in what your character discovered earlier. If you need help, do what one of my clients did. He played with his 5-year-old son to help him reconnect to his childlike self. Through this, he was able to discover his true self and his passions. Do whatever is fun for you to connect to your childlike self so that you can uncover what you like to do.

Some questions I asked myself that you can ask yourself:

- What do I want to learn?

- Where do I want to travel?

- What is important to me?

- How do you want the following to look in your life?

  o Career

  o Friends

  o Spiritual

o   Fun

o   Health/Fitness

o   Relationships

o   Spirituality

o   Other

- What classes can you take that will light your soul on fire?

CHAPTER 3

"V" ~ Value, Appreciate and honor Who You Are Every Day

O K, NOW THAT YOU HAVE DONE all of the hard work in Chapters 1 and 2, it is about remembering to stay in love with yourself. Here are some easy ways to do this:

- **Celebrate everything daily by keeping a journal.** We all do so much every day that we forget to acknowledge ourselves. Journaling for me was such a big way to see so much more of me and all that I do. It helped me really honor, love and respect myself. You can include any or all of the following and anything else you want to add:

- ○ What did you do for you today?
- ○ How did you take care of your loved ones?
- ○ How did you honor your health, your spirituality?
- ○ What did you do to help a stranger?
- ○ What did you do great in your job/business?
- ○ What else was awesome about you today?

- **Create a celebration board** – all of the things that you are so proud of that you have accomplished in your life

- **Create a gratitude board** – everything in your life that you are grateful for right now

- **Write a love letter to yourself** – what do you love about yourself? So often, we are so good about telling others what we love about them, but forget to tell ourselves what we love about ourselves.

- **Presence** – remember to stay present and grounded in each moment with yourself and whoever you are with. You are exactly where you are meant to be.

- **Gratitude** – continue to remember everything that you have to be grateful for each day.

CHAPTER 4

"e" – Enjoy and Express you

I N LOVING OURSELVES, we can be free to fully express who we are. The world needs all of us. Cookie cutter people running around are BOR – ING ☺!! So how can you express YOU? To help you think of ideas, here are some things I did:

• **Have Fun/Play** I discovered what is fun for me and I went out and did it. I even brought my hula hoop to business meetings. Remember to bring out that childlike part of you. A friend and I went to the zoo and we pretended that we were 10 years old. We ran around and enjoyed the zoo like kids would. It was awesome!

Marcy Hula Hooping at Business Meeting

○ I developed a *Play to Discover Your Passion* Workshop and expressed my *Tinkerangel* self. What can you create to express yourself?

○ I express my real self on social media and guess what – it is refreshing. It liberates me and it inspires others to do the same. People tell me all the time how much they appreciate that I am not afraid to be me and it helps give them the freedom to do the same.

- **More Fun/Play Ideas**
    - How about having a birthday party or choose any other time of year where you can truly celebrate you? Create posters and post them all around the party space. Have others bring stories of why they appreciate you. Woohoo – there is a lot to celebrate!

    - Make playdates with yourself or invite other fun people to go on playdates with you.

    - Marry yourself. I know that sounds crazy but how about making some vows with yourself around how you are going to honor, cherish and love yourself for the rest of your life? When I married my ex-husband and we were exchanging vows, I accidently said "I marry myself Marcy." OMG, I was so horrified and embarrassed by the mistake I made in front of everyone at our wedding. In reflection, I thought, *wait – isn't that what we should really do – marry, honor, and love ourselves first?* I say yes – it is.

    - What other ways can you celebrate you?

Now it's time to go share the love with others – help people everywhere learn to love themselves – and from that – the world will truly be a happier place filled with love ☺.

HERE'S TO LOVING OURSELVES UNCONDI-
TIONALLY AND IN TURN UNCONDITIONAL-
LY LOVING OTHERS IN A MUCH DEEPER AND
PROFOUND WAY.

END NOTE

Tinkerangel's Vision

I envision a new world where creative, fun play is the acceptable way of being. Where everyone is encouraged to live their passion and purpose, and in doing this we all work together to create world change. This world is one where there is abundance for all and it is a world filled with unconditional love, helping each other, collaborating and sharing, full of joy, peace, compassion, empathy, deep listening, authenticity, flow, spontaneity, freedom, simplicity, community, harmony, stillness, nature, adventure, laughter and childlike wonderment. Will you join me in this new world? I would love to hear from you about your journey of falling in love with YOU and anything else that you would like to share.

Please feel free to email me at marcy@tinkerangel.com.

Resources

- Amanda Meisner, DNA Activation Specialist/ Energy Work, amandameisner1@gmail.com
- Barbara Korte, Spiritual Counselor who uses energy/sound and direction from Spirit to guide you to clear and align your physical, mental, emotional and spiritual bodies and integrate any pieces of your life that have been neglected or broken off, bringing one into empowerment and wholeness. www.intheheartofsedona.com, higherpath@hotmail.com.
- Cheryl Angela, Vibrational Catalyst, Transformational Coach and Visionary Musician, www.cherylangela.com, cherylangela99@gmail.com
- Donna Pinto, Book Editor, dp4peace@yahoo.com
- Jesse Gros, Coach, www.insightadventures.com, www.jessegros.com, jesse_gros@yahoo.com
- Joseph White Wolf, Spiritual Teacher, josephwhitewolf@hotmail.com
- Marcy Morrison, Career and Life Weaving, www.careerswithwings.com, marcy@careerswithwithwings.com
- Natalie Vail, L.Ac. Dipl.O.M, owns and operates an alternative health and wellness practice in San Diego called Soulistic Total Health. She is a licensed Acupuncturist who possesses a wide range of

training and natural gifts and therefore creates a "one-stop holistic shop" for her clients. Best known for her work as an intuitive counselor and certified psychic-medium, she is also a very experienced energy healer, Chinese herbalist, and classical Feng Shui consultant. www.natalievail.com, NatVail-CA@gmail.com.

MARCY'S FUN PLAYFUL BIOGRAPHY

Marcy Morrison, aka Tinkerangel, (tinkerangel.com) is a career and life weaver. She does this work through her company Careers with Wings (careerswithwings.com). Marcy envisions a world where people live their passion and purpose and everyone works together to create world change. Marcy is the author of *Finding Your Passion: The Easy Guide to Your Dream Career*, a book which helps people along this path.

After experiencing the traditional career path, Marcy discovered that that is not why she is here. She knows that she is here to play her Tinkerangel role of sprinkling joy and happy dust on others so they can live their passion and purpose, as well as wrapping her wings around others to support them on their journey. Marcy lives in San Diego with her two boys Cameron and Logan, who she plays with as much as possible. Originally from the Jersey Shore, Marcy considers herself a wannabe Latina. She speaks Spanish and has worked, lived and studied all over the world. Marcy's serious credentials (blah, blah, blah…) can be found here: careerswithwings.com.

Made in the USA
San Bernardino, CA
01 March 2014